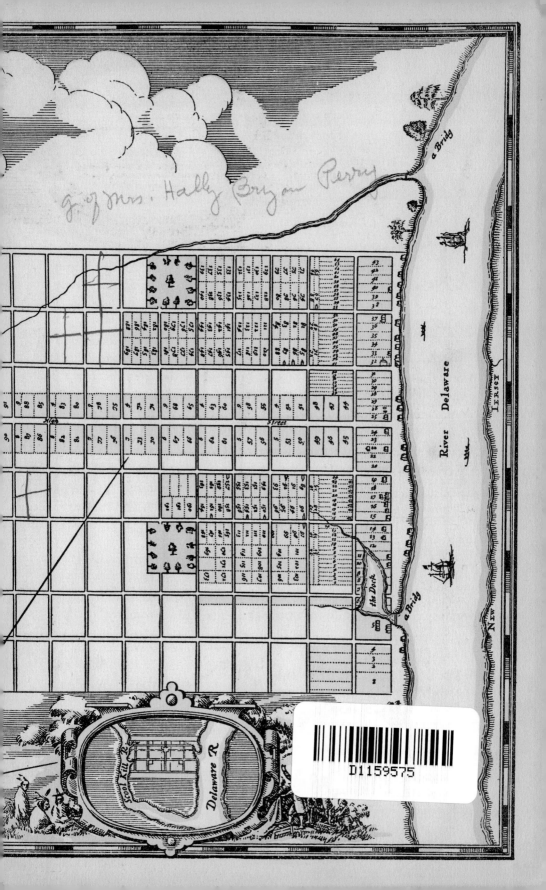

EXCERPTS *from*

A Letter from *William Penn*, Proprietary Governour
of *PENNSYLVANIA*, &c.

My Kind Friends:

THE Kindnefs of yours by the Ship *Thomas* and *Anne*, doth much oblige me; for by it I perceive the Interest you take in my *Health* and *Reputation*, and the *profperous Beginnings* of this *Province*, which you are fo kind as to think may much depend upon them.

XXXII. *Philadelphia*, the Expectation of thofe that are concern'd in this *Province*, if at laft *laid out* to the great Content of those here, that are any wayes Interefted therein; the *Scituation* is a Neck of Land, and lieth between two Navigable Rivers, *Delaware* and *Skulkill*, whereby it hath two Fronts upon the Water, each a *Mile* and *two* from River to River. *Delaware* is a glorious River, but the *Skulkill* being an *hundred Miles* Boatable above the *Falls*, and its Courfe *North-East* toward the Fountain of *Sufquahannah* (that tends to the Heart of the Province, and both fides our own) it is like to be a great part of the Settlement of this Age.

* * * * * * because I believe you have been entertained with this and fome other profitable Subjects by your Prefident, I fhall add no more, but to affure you, that I am heartily inclined to advance your juft Interest, and that you will always find me

Your Kind Cordial Friend,

Philadelphia, the 16th of the
6th Moneth, call'd *Auguft*
1683.

William Penn

ONE HUNDRED YEARS

Independence Hall, America's most treasured landmark and the cradle of her liberty, was long guarded by a "Franklin" policy.

ONE HUNDRED YEARS:

BY JEROME B. GRAY

BEING

A SHORT HISTORY OF FIRES, *and the* METH-
ODS OF FIGHTING FIRES *during the* PAST
ONE HUNDRED YEARS;

Together with some INTERESTING FACTS *about*
Fires of ancient Times;

REPRODUCTIONS *of* ETCHINGS *of* HISTORI-
CAL BUILDINGS *in* Philadelphia *and* many
little Drawings *of* old Fire Apparatus *and*
the House Marks *of* Fire Companies;

Also a BRIEF STORY *of the* Founding *and* Growth
of the FRANKLIN FIRE INSURANCE COM-
PANY *in* Philadelphia.

PHILADELPHIA

MCMXXIX

The Franklin Fire Insurance Company
of Philadelphia

FOREWORD

*A*PRIL 22, 1929, *concludes One Hundred Years of uninterrupted progress for The Franklin Fire Insurance Company, Philadelphia. But April 22, 1929, has a still greater significance—for that same date also inaugurates the Second Century of that progress!*

Thus, though we look forward optimistically to a future prosperity, we realize that its attainment depends on the solidity of the foundation laid in the century now completed.

Throughout the pages of this book, the history of The Franklin Fire Insurance Company has been intentionally subdued to make room for the broader import of a brief and sketch-like history of the development of fire-fighting methods in Philadelphia and for a record of a few of the many fascinating highlights in that development.

"One Hundred Years" is presented to you with the compliments of the company whose experience has made its publication possible. Accept it, then, as a memento of the past, a reflection of the present and an indication of the future.

7

One Hundred Years

The EARLY HISTORY *of* FIRE FIGHTING *and* FIRE PREVENTION, *together with some* Interesting Facts *about its* Development *during the last* ONE HUNDRED YEARS

NO fire ever blazed that was more replete with thrills and interest than the glowing sparks that fly from the history of its prevention and suppression, for that history is in turn a romance and a paradox. It is a romance because it is chock-full of the most amusing and amazing human incidents; it is a paradox because, like architecture, it early reached a high point of practical and intelligent development only later to pass through a period of retrogression during which it was obvious that no serious attention was being given it.

A romance and a paradox

The lack of attention, however, particularly in the early days of Philadelphia history, was undoubtedly due more to a lack of serious conflagrations than to any careless disregard of the theoretical need of fire-fighting equipment. To put it in the modern vernacular, Philadelphians had not become fire-conscious. Thus, it

9

is perhaps pardonable, even though Philadelphia had been named, surveyed, planted and lots had begun to be occupied by settlers in July of 1682, that no public measures were taken for the extinguishment of fires until May 25, 1695.

The Fire Brigade of Imperial Rome EVEN so—to dig deeper into history—those who repeatedly stress the wonders of progress and who hold firmly to the belief that each new day brings the world closer to an elusive perfection, might be embarrassed if they were asked to explain why the prevention of fire was nothing short of primitive in this country until the Eighteenth Century, while Imperial Rome, as early as the reign of Cæsar Augustus in 732 B. C., enjoyed the protection of a fire brigade consisting of seven cohorts of one thousand men each!

As a matter of additional fact, the Fire Brigade of Imperial Rome, in principle and practice, was not far behind the fire departments of modern cities one hundred years ago: In certain districts of the city, brigades of fire fighters were barracked, ever ready to respond to the bucina, a large trumpet-like horn that would be blown at the first sign of a blaze by fire guardians or sentinels stationed in high towers surrounding the city.

At the first sound from the bucina, the Roman firemen would hasten to the scene of the fire, equipped with ladders, axes, buckets, hammers, saws, mattocks, leather hose and even with a large "water squirt" on wheels. The fire was under the direction of a Fire Centurion who corresponded to the modern Fire Chief but who, instead of dashing to the fire in a speeding red automobile, arrived in a special chariot drawn by four white horses.

THAT the Roman municipal fire department *The first fire* should be equipped with a "water squirt" on *engine* wheels—history also records that it was equipped with large pillows which were used as we now use nets, and with sectionalized ladders little different from those of today—gives some indication of the high point of fire-

fighting development reached before the Christian Era. Pliny referred to fire engines, and Herod of Alexandria, in his treatise on pneumatics in 150 B. C., describes the oldest known engine as "the siphons used in conflagrations." And siphons they were, pumped by hand and filled by the cohorts with vases full of water.

But Rome, perhaps, even in 732 B. C., cannot be justly compared to the Philadelphia of 1695—and it may be (we approach this timidly) that the youthful City of Brotherly Love did not do as the Romans had done because it was not in Rome! In 1695, however, the inhabitants petitioned the Governor and Council to pass a law providing them with ladders and leather buckets.

SUCH a demand could not go unheeded, because it was generally agreed by this time that the growing community was continually threatened by fire. To propose the provision of ladders and leather buckets, and actually to provide them, however, had no more similarity than a conflagration and a false alarm. Money was scarce and both the Governor and Council were agreed that neither ladders nor leather buckets could be supplied merely for the asking. With an instinctive political move, therefore, the logical solution, since the inhabitants requested equipment, was to make the inhabitants finance its purchase. Thus, with a bill passed by the Provincial Legislature in 1696, one finds the city's earliest fire prevention centering more upon the legislature of inhabitants than upon legislation *for* equipment. *The Provincial Legislature passes a law*

THIS bill prohibited people from cleaning their chimneys by burning them out, yet forbade foul chimneys under a penalty of forty shillings. It further provided that each inhabitant must keep at his dwelling *No smoking in the streets*

13

a "swab, twelve or fourteen feet long, and a bucket or pail, to be ready in case of accident by fire, under penalty of ten shillings." As a further precaution, no one was allowed to smoke in the streets by day or night, under penalty of twelve pence, or to keep more than six pounds of gunpowder "within forty perches of any dwelling."

How the abstinence from smoking in the streets and the prevalence of smoking in the houses could possibly curb the familiar sight of burning chimneys is not even dimly recorded!

The Ordinance of 1713
THOUGH the law was passed with the best intentions—as evidenced by the fact that all fines paid to the Justices of the Peace were used for the purchase of leather buckets, hooks and ladders—a similar law, passed in 1700, requiring each householder to keep two leather buckets, and a re-enactment in 1702, directing the magistrates to procure "six or eight good hooks for tearing down houses on fire," made unpopular the bill of 1696. Thus, on August 14, 1713, one finds the passing of an ordinance which said, in part: "It being very difficult to convict such as suffer their chimneys to take fire, contrary to a law of this Province, it is therefore

ordered that if the offender will pay the forfeiture without further trouble, he shall have ten shillings abated him."

Gradually, therefore, under the pressure of the Provincial Legislature, each household was becoming a miniature though primitive fire company of its own. Any attempt at organized companies had not been made and, indeed, it is doubtful that they had even been considered. Fire engines or any kind of a machine for fire fighting was unknown in the country. It seemed sufficient, in view of the comparatively insignificant blazes of these early years, that each household be well supplied with buckets. And well supplied they were, even long after the introduction of fire engines.

ONE man, however, realized that the fires of small importance at least gave evidence of their possibilities to develop into conflagrations, and that their insignificance was doubtless due more to good luck than to good management. This man was Samuel Preston, the Mayor, who, in 1711, told the Board of Council that he had frequently had in his consideration "the many providences this city has met with, in that fires, that have so often happened, have done so little dam-

Samuel Preston speaks to the Board of Council

15

age." He recommended, therefore, that steps be taken forthwith to purchase efficient equipment as preparedness against the "lusty blaze" that seemed to him inevitable.

Though no serious fires had happened up to this time, the city had grown until its skyline revealed about seven hundred dwellings, reason enough to give added weight to Mayor Preston's recommendation. Fires were small and infrequent, but they were inevitably destructive because of the primitive methods of fighting them.

The sounding of a fire alarm and the call for buckets

WHEN a fire was discovered at night, for instance, the watchman sprang his rattle, a contrivance having a tongue playing on the teeth of a ratchet wheel which, when revolved, produced a series of sharp, staccato noises. The watchman would then run around the town, like a demounted Paul Revere, knock at the doors of all the dwelling houses and cry loudly: "Throw out your buckets!" The general confusion caused by the watchman's rattle and his significant order, together with the ringing of bells which spread the alarm, soon had the householders aroused and dressing hurriedly to fulfill their duties as firemen.

WHEN A FIRE WAS DISCOVERED
AT NIGHT, THE WATCHMAN
SPRANG HIS RATTLE.

17

The first duty of those early Philadelphians was to obey the watchman's order by throwing their leather buckets into the street. These buckets were required to be hung in the passage of each house, close to the street door. They were made of sole leather, each of approximately the same size, with a capacity of three gallons of water. Each, too, was marked with its owner's name, for reasons that we shall presently see.

The fighting of a fire AS the buckets were tossed into the streets, they were picked up by those speedier dressers who were already hastening to the fire. As a consequence—and for a reason that is not particularly obvious—the fire was fought by householders with their neighbors' buckets. Thus, after the fire had been extinguished, the buckets were thrown on any nearby lot and the Town Crier cried: "Hear ye, Oh, I pray ye, claim your buckets!" Little imagination is required to picture the result: With the fire extinguished and with no light to guide them, unless the fire had occurred providently and simultaneously with a full moon, the ensuing scramble for buckets made a college flour fight tame in comparison. To augment a disturbance that was invariably sufficient in itself, the signal from the Town Crier gener-

18

AS THE BUCKETS WERE
TOSSED INTO THE STREETS,
THEY WERE PICKED UP BY
THOSE WHO WERE HASTEN-
ING TO THE FIRE.

ally brought the boys from all parts of the town, each
eager to get the buckets of the rich, since the boys who
brought those prizes home were usually rewarded. We
see, then, that our earlier inhabitants were not satisfied
with the mere thrill of a fire, and that the blaze itself
was merely the excuse for a general orgy of fisticuffs,
rioting, battered heads and cauliflower ears—all for the
sake of sole-leather buckets!

19

At the fire, two lines were formed from the fire to the nearest pump or well. When either the pump or the well had been emptied of water, the line was extended to the next pump or well or, if necessary, down to the river itself. It was the duty of one line to pass up full buckets from the source of supply to the blaze; of the other line to pass back the empty buckets. It was an endless chain arrangement that was effective enough at

THE FIRE WAS FORGOTTEN IN THE APPARENTLY MORE PRESSING MATTER OF DELUGING THE SLACKER.

small blazes, but as ineffective at a conflagration as the same system applied to an attempt to drain the ocean.

NO one was permitted to break through these lines. *How slackers* If he attempted to do so, and would not fall in and *were* lend a hand, the fire was instantly forgotten in the ap- *received* parently more pressing matter of deluging the slacker with the contents of as many buckets as could be emptied upon him before he could escape into the night. History shows that these dramatic little by-plays were by no means exceptions to the rule, and that many small fires, at the point of being subdued, gained fresh headway under these sudden "breaks in the hose"!

SEVEN years after the picturesque recommendation *Philadelphia* of Samuel Preston to the Board of Council, Phila- *buys her first* delphia purchased her first fire engine; and on Decem- *fire engine* ber 8, 1718, we find Council issuing the following statement: "The Council having agreed with one Abraham Bickley for his fire engine at the sum of fifty pounds, it is ordered that the Treasurer pay ye said sum out of ye money raised or to be raised for chimney-firing with all expedition possible."

Since the ordinance of 1713, five years earlier, had already been a public admission of the difficulty of convicting "such as suffer their chimneys to take fire," one may well wonder at the optimism of Abraham Bickley in accepting such hazardous terms. Nevertheless, he accepted them and delivered his engine—a curiosity that attracted the entire populace of the city. Bickley was paid on December 19, 1719, over a year after the purchase. He was not paid, however, from the fines imposed on the townspeople, but from a fund appropriated to provide an engine house for the machine that was rapidly deteriorating after twelve months of no protection.

A public chimney sweep WITH the Bickley engine purchased, there doubtless were many who now wished for a good blaze on which to test its merits. But the town's impressive novelty seemed, even by its presence, to destroy all signs of fire. What fires there were usually gave up in a thin trail of blue-gray smoke under the urge of the bucket brigade before the heavy apparatus could be rumbled over the cobbles of the streets to the scene of the blaze; and three years after its acquisition, in January of 1721, we find the appointment of James Henderson as a public chimney sweep. Henderson was probably considered a more valuable addition to the fire-fighting equipment

Cherry street, the oldest remaining Colonial street in Philadelphia, preserving much of the quaintness and charm of early Philadelphia.

than either the "swab, twelve or fourteen feet long" that each inhabitant, "under penalty of ten shillings," was required to keep at his dwelling, or the Bickley engine.

IN December, 1726, eight years after its purchase, *Mr. Claypole* the Bickley fire engine was reported out of repair *takes his job* and a Committee of Aldermen was commissioned to *seriously* view it and to make whatever recommendations they saw fit. But committees worked leisurely even in 1726, and it was not until July, 1729, that we find any action being given to their findings. Then, however, a townsman by the name of George Claypole was employed at an annual salary of three pounds to keep the city engine in good repair and to make monthly trials of it. Mr. Claypole took his job seriously—so seriously, in fact, that he promptly resigned after one month and happily relinquished his post to Richard Armitt, who was employed to replace him.

BUT the Bickley fire engine was not much longer *The fire on* to be idle, for in 1730 the first serious fire in Phila- *Fishbourne's* delphia kept the citizens and that engine fighting with *Wharf* their backs to the wall, not to save a single dwelling or to extinguish a lone chimney, but to conquer a fire which threatened the entire city. The fire broke out on Fishbourne's Wharf, below Walnut Street, crossed Water Street and burned the buildings of Jonathan Dickson, valued at five thousand pounds. In addition to the ravages of the fire, Philadelphia now had her first taste of looting as one other situation to cope with in her future program of fire protection, for this fire in 1730 proved beyond question of doubt that Philadelphians were not all honest, and that some citizens, supposedly fighting the conflagration, had occupied themselves energetically with tasks that, though dishonest, were more profitable than passing buckets or manning the Bickley engine. Commenting on this phase of the Fishbourne Wharf fire, *The Fireman's Record*, published in 1892 as a memento of the Fireman's Pension Fund, observed casually: "This looting was a new proof of the immorality which was spreading."

The city of
1730
PHILADELPHIA was no longer a tiny settlement in 1730. Records show that during this year 171 vessels cleared her port, 161 vessels entered, 622 votes were cast and 227 deaths occurred. The fire might actually have done more good than harm, for behind the

24

ruins lay the determination of many citizens to demand more efficient fire-fighting equipment in preparation for the next fire that they realized to be inevitable. When the fire had finally been extinguished, the need of fire-fighting equipment was more a topic of conversation than the relation of harrowing experiences or the expression of sympathy for those whose loss was greatest. Indeed, Jonathan Dickson was the only recipient of public sympathy, for William Fishbourne, ex-Mayor, man of many trusts and trustee of the Loan Office, had been declared a defaulter when two thousand pounds of the public funds had disappeared during his office.

IT was now palpable, however, that additional fire *Engines,* apparatus was necessary; and in April, 1730, the city *buckets,* ordered three more engines, 400 leather buckets, 20 *ladders,* ladders and 25 hooks. One of the engines was to be *hooks* made in Philadelphia by Anthony Nichols; the other two were ordered from London. In order that the expense might not fall too heavily on the citizens, it was proposed that a subscription be raised and it was ordered that a tax of two pence per pound and eight shillings per head be forthwith laid on the townspeople.

The two engines and 250 leather buckets arrived from England in January, 1731. The balance of the buckets were made in Philadelphia from a sample produced by Thomas Oldman. The home-made product seemed every bit as good as those imported from abroad, and they were purchased, with a vague gesture of civic pride, for nine shillings each. In January, 1733, the Nichols' Philadelphia-made fire engine was ready and tested. One of the Philadelphia papers of the day, commenting on the test, said: "It played the water much higher than those purchased from London."

Philadelphia houses her three fire engines and thinks more seriously of fire prevention

AND now, with three engines on hand—the original Bickley engine had been discarded shortly after the great fire of 1730—there arose the question of housing them. This was decided after due deliberation by the Board of Council, and one of the engines was stationed in a corner of the Great Meeting-House Yard, southwest corner of High and Second Streets; the other in Francis Jones' lot, corner of Front and Walnut Streets; and the third in a corner of the Baptist Meeting Yard, Second Street near Arch. The leather buckets were hung in the Court House. The city, at last, seemed to be giving some serious attention to the business of

fighting fires; and from this point on we see a much
faster development, possibly for two very significant
reasons: One, the rapid growth of the city was increasing fire hazards; two, intelligent men with the prophetic vision that builds cities were thinking and talk-
ing fire prevention.

27

ONE of these men was none other than Benjamin Franklin who had already become one of Philadelphia's illustrious patriots and one of her most important citizens through his writings, his *Pennsylvania Gazette*, his scientific research and his profound philosophy on the economic conditions of his country and his city. The other was a well-known citizen named Anthony Atwood, who, in Franklin's *Pennsylvania Gazette* of February 4, 1735, and above the initials, "A. A.," had written a communication in reference to fires, advising the immediate formation of fire companies which would alleviate the riots and fool's play of the then existing fire-fighting methods, and claiming that there was "not enough water to keep the pumps going for a half hour together."

SHORTLY after Franklin's publication of this significant communication—and there can be no question that Franklin was not of the same opinion as Anthony Atwood—the houses of Budd's Long Row, Front Street above the Drawbridge, took fire and threatened the destruction of a large amount of property. Though the equipment of the city, as we have seen, had been increased by three engines and many additional buckets, hooks and ladders, the difficulty with which this fire was finally brought under control proved again that the city was by no means equipped to save itself from a general conflagration in the event that one occurred. There were further suggestions made by the press and by several of the leading citizens, but the recommendation of forming fire companies seemed now to predominate and it was obvious that the publicly printed suggestions of Franklin and Atwood were making themselves felt.

CHARACTERISTIC of Benjamin Franklin, typical of the man's ability to bring to a practical development anything whose theoretical possibilities seemed to warrant such development, history does not surprise us when it records that, on December 7, 1736, through Benjamin Franklin's effort, interest and enthusiasm, Philadelphia's first fire company was founded. Perhaps, too, it did not surprise the citizens of Philadelphia at that time, for Franklin was always doing the most astonishing things; and in one of his earliest letters on fire prevention is found the famous epigram that has since been applied to everything from pills to investments and from advertising to insurance policies—"An ounce of prevention is worth a pound of

The Union Fire Company, Philadelphia's first, is founded

" . . . LIVING FIRE-BRANDS
OR COALS IN A FULL SHOVEL
. . . SHOULD BE CONTAINED
IN A WARMING PAN AND
SHUT . . ."

cure." Had he not advised, also, that "living fire-brands
or coals in a full shovel to be carried from one room to
another or up and down stairs should be contained in a
warming pan and shut, for scraps of fire might fall into
crevices and make no appearance until midnight, when
your stairs being in flames, you might be forced to leap

out of the window and hazard a broken neck in order to avoid being over-roasted"? Had he not, too, advised the passage of a law forbidding shallow hearths and "the detestable practice of placing wooden moldings on the sides of the fireplaces"?

The name of this first company was the Union Fire Company. It was located on Grindstone Alley, and those who actually sat together at its founding were Benjamin Franklin, Isaac Paschal, Samuel Powell, William Rawle and Samuel Syme.

The Union Fire Company was purely voluntary, an association for mutual assistance with a membership limited to thirty. In accordance with the constitution—which, by the way, furnished the model until long after the Revolutionary War for the many companies that came into existence in such rapid succession thereafter —each member agreed to furnish, at his own expense, six leather buckets and two strong linen bags, each marked conspicuously with his own name and the name of the company. The use for the leather buckets needs no further explanation; the linen bags were provided to hold property in danger and to save it from theft— the first tangible result of the lesson learned at the Fishbourne Wharf fire six years earlier.

LINEN BAGS WERE PRO-
VIDED TO HOLD PROPERTY
IN DANGER AND TO SAVE
IT FROM THEFT.

*"The mem-
bers had
different
duties"* THE members of the Union Fire Company had different duties, arranged and interchanged at their
regular meetings. Each member, of course, had to at-
tend each fire and to reach each fire as quickly as his

32

legs or his ingenuity could carry him. At the fire, some would superintend the use of water, others would stand at the doors of houses which were in the danger zone, to protect them from the looters who had by now become as familiar at a fire as flames and smoke. On an alarm of fire at night, it was agreed that lights should be placed in the windows of the houses of members near the fire, "in order to prevent confusion and to enable friends to give more speedy and effectual assistance."

Eight meetings of the Union Fire Company were held annually. A supper costing three shillings was served at each meeting. Members who came late were fined one shilling; those who failed to report at all were fined four shillings. There was a treasurer, but no president, of the company. Each member served in turn as a clerk for one month. His duties were not severe: he merely notified his associates of the next meeting, inspected their leather buckets and linen bags and, when these were not in good order, reported the fact to the company. Engines and buckets were the only available apparatus, for pumps were few during these years and water was scarce. But the Union Fire Company did memorable work during its existence and remained active until 1820.

SUCH A RIVALRY GREW BETWEEN THEM THAT THEY FOUGHT EACH OTHER WITH AS MUCH GUSTO AS THEY FOUGHT THE FLAMES.

Benjamin Franklin starts a new idea

AS usual with Benjamin Franklin, what he established and accomplished almost invariably produced a series of similar endeavors. It is ever thus with pioneers who possess the foresight to create and the fortitude to give their creations actual form. Naturally, then, we find other fire companies springing up with the alacrity of the flames they were founded to quell. Space here is too limited to permit even a brief record of all of these, they came so rapidly. But they were welcome and, though such a rivalry grew between them that they fought each other with as much gusto as they fought the flames, they laid the foundation for

34

fire prevention that gave no further fear of the city's whole destruction.

COLORFUL, those early days when the volunteer fire companies were in turn the protection and the terror of a city. Riots and heroism, fisticuffs and helping hands—all played a part on the same blazing stage. But the rioting had a habit occasionally of occupying more of the firemen's attention than the flames; so the Board of Council was finally compelled to pass another ordinance. This document attacked the difficulties from many angles, with section after section aimed at the betterment of conditions that by this time had become intolerable. A committee was appointed, whose duty it was to visit the different companies, inspect their apparatus and inquire into their condition and conduct, reporting its findings to the Council.

Riots and the attempt to stop them

This apparently proved an ineffective remedy, however, for we read later that "riots and outrages being still perpetrated by the fire companies, councils declared the need of concentrated action between the city and districts, which were divided into three districts: southern district, consisting of Southwark, Moyamensing, adjoining districts, and adjacent towns; middle district, Philadelphia and West Philadelphia; northern district, Northern Liberties, Spring Garden, and adjoining townships."

Only by the request of authorized persons were the city companies permitted to pass into adjoining districts. The use of fire plugs was regulated, and minors were forbidden to join companies. The companies were required to make annual reports to councils and "to present two persons to councils, from whom councils should appoint one from each company, to form a board, which, under direction of councils, had general supervision of fires." The mayor had the power of removal, and penalty was provided for riotous and disorderly conduct.

But again, failure; and finally the authority of the legislature was invoked to prohibit rioting at fires and to provide methods of forming new companies, subject to the approval of the court.

The second Philadelphia fire company —and others THE Fellowship Fire Company was Philadelphia's second. It was founded on New Year's Day of 1738, and was located on a lot belonging to the Friend's Meeting, on Second Street near Market. Not enjoying a house of its own, the Fellowship equipment was in

36

evidence at various amusing places throughout the city. Fire ladders, for instance, were kept under the eaves of the butchers' shambles. But the company was founded with determination, did splendid fire-fighting and rioting and survived until 1825.

Next came the Hand-In-Hand Fire Company, founded on March 1, 1742, and located on the northeast corner of Sixth and Walnut Streets. Considering its membership as a whole, this company was easily the most illustrious, for it was composed of most of the eminent Philadelphians of the period, among them physicians, lawyers, clergymen, scientists and citizens of wealth and refinement. The early history of the Hand-In-Hand is vague because the company's minutes between December, 1796, and May, 1816, were lost. It is known, however, that the company became proficient fire fighters in every sense of the word at that time, and that it ceased to be active in 1816 when age and its attendant infirmities had made the members grow careless of their duties.

There then followed, at rather regular intervals, the founding of the Heart-In-Hand Fire Company (February 22, 1743), the Friendship Fire Company (July 30, 1747), the Star Fire Company (January 4, 1749), the Brittania Fire Company (1750-1751), the Hibernia Fire Company (February 20, 1752), the Franklin Fire Company (1792), and so on and on through the progress of Philadelphia years.

Hand-in-Hand or Hibernia? IT would be interesting to record a few of the highlights in the history of each of these companies, but they were essentially the same in their constitutions, each patterned unmistakably after that so capably developed by Benjamin Franklin and his associates for the Union Fire Company.

Though it will be seen from the partial list we have given—and we have every reason to believe that our sources of information were chronologically reliable—the Hand-In-Hand Fire Company was founded on March 1, 1742, and the Hibernia Fire Company was founded on February 20, 1752, nearly ten years later. Despite this difference, however, the Hibernia had a long dispute with the Hand-In-Hand about which should enjoy the distinction of being founded first. The dispute became so energetic that an alarm of fire was regarded simultaneously as the starting gong for a lively and bloody combat between the two companies. It was thought best, therefore, to settle the dispute in court.

38

The house in which Benjamin Franklin is supposed to have lived. It is protected from fire by the company that bears his name.

Oddly enough, historical calendar dates to the contrary notwithstanding, the court decided in favor of Hibernia! The grounds for this decision were that the Hand-In-Hand Fire Company had kept no minutes at the time of its alleged organization. In other words, there was no record of organization until the company had been in business for several years.

The Northern Liberty Fire Company, founded four years after the Hibernia Fire Company, had the distinction both of being the first fire company formed outside of the city proper and also of having as one of its members, Mr. Richard Mason. The company was located on the Northeast corner of Cable Lane and Callowhill Street; Mr. Richard Mason was the first successful builder of fire engines in this country.

The Brittania Fire Company went out of service at the beginning of the Revolutionary War, doubtless because of the unhappy choice of its name and of the decided unpopularity of that name. The King George Fire Company and the Queen Charlotte Fire Company, however, decided that the service they were founded to provide was of more importance than their names, so they merely changed their names to Delaware Fire Company and Fame Fire Company, respectively.

39

IN 1791, regardless of the fact that the city's fire companies had been augmented by the addition of three new ones—Relief Fire Company, Diligent Fire Company and Kensington Fire Company—Philadelphia was visited by its most serious conflagration when a fire broke out in Hamilton's Buildings at the Drawbridge, completely destroyed several stores and all their contents and left a toll of death of twelve firemen killed by falling walls.

In this same year, shortly after the Hamilton fire, a livery stable on Dock Street near Third Street caught fire, spread to other buildings, mostly wood, and completely destroyed twenty houses before it was brought under control. For a time it was feared that this whole section of the city was lost. There was no loss of life in this fire, but the ruins left pathetic suffering among the poor. To relieve this until that part of the city could build up again, a committee was appointed to collect a subscription and a benefit was given at the old theatre on South Street.

Fires, fires, fires! One has a feeling that little tongues of flame lay hidden in that early Philadelphia to leap out without a moment's warning to laugh at the human efforts to prevent them.

40

FIRE INSURANCE BEGINS *to* OCCUPY *the* MINDS *of*
WELL-KNOWN PHILADELPHIANS *and the* CITIZENS
are FINALLY ASKED *to* SUBSCRIBE *to the* ARTICLES
of INSURANCE.

D URING this period in which Philadelphia was *Benjamin*
witnessing the almost annual founding of a new *Franklin*
fire company, Benjamin Franklin was busying his mind *dreams of*
another form
with the practical development of yet another form of *of fire*
fire protection—a form of protection that had already *protection*
had his serious consideration in a publication issued in
1725 and entitled, "Ways and Means for the Inhabitants of Delaware to Become Rich." This was the first
book published in America relating to insurance, and
insurance, of course, figuratively speaking, was that
other form of fire protection.

With conditions as they were; with fires consuming
the property of Philadelphians who were financially
unable to rebuild and who, in most cases, lost everything
when they lost the roof above their heads; and with the
necessity of taking up public subscriptions and of giving
benefits at the theatres to relieve the suffering of those

41

whom the gods of fire had visited, one needs but little imagination to picture Franklin's thoughts about insurance. "Here are inhabitants of my own city," he seems to say, "who know no help in the event of fire consuming their properties. There must assuredly be some method by which many people could pay a small sum of money to protect their properties, the assurance being that a certain sum would be awarded them in case of fire. Those who are not visited by fire, but who likewise contributed to such a fund, would pay the monies necessary to take care of losses; but even so, they should be consoled in the thought that they have the same protection as the less fortunate ones, and that others' monies would likewise pay their losses."

The first fire insurance company

THOUGH Benjamin Franklin was thinking of fire insurance in these early years, and though the crystallization of his thoughts was being published by himself and influencing many other prominent Philadelphians to think seriously of the same thing, February 18, 1752, had come before the citizens were asked to subscribe to the Articles of Insurance. Two months later, on April 13, 1752, the first fire insurance company of America was started. This was known, is known

42

today, as the Philadelphia Contributionship, a name that is now rich in tradition and experience. Benjamin Franklin was the first to subscribe to the new company and was, fittingly enough, chosen as its first director.

U NDOUBTEDLY, the most interesting phase of this company's early history—and one, furthermore, that had a direct effect in causing the formation of Philadelphia's second fire insurance company—was its definite business policy of insuring only those houses which were not surrounded by trees. This policy was adopted on account of the difficulties of getting water to the fire through foliage and overhanging branches, and also because of the belief that trees attracted lightning and thus made the risk needlessly severe. Today, of course, there are, theoretically, no obstacles between a fire department and a fire, but today is not 1752, when fire apparatus was little short of primitive and when the water supply was scant. *Trees and water and lightning*

T HE policy adopted by the Philadelphia Contributionship was taken as a matter of course during the company's early years, probably because the citizens had nothing with which to draw the mental comparisons so much a part of mental conclusions. But as the years *How the "Green Tree" grew*

43

grew on and the fire apparatus became palpably more efficient, and as it began to dawn on the owners of tree-shaded houses that numerous thunderstorms had come and gone and that their houses had not yet been fired by lightning, these people began to wonder why, after all, the virtues of fire insurance should be denied them. Consequently, in 1784, we find the inauguration of the Mutual Assurance Company, significantly known as the "Green Tree."

The Mutual Assurance Company specialized in the insurance of houses surrounded by trees. It had to. There was none of the other prospects left. But the company advanced cautiously in its issuance of policies, requiring a deposit of twenty shillings more than that required by the Philadelphia Contributionship, and demanding that all trees surrounding an insured house must be kept trimmed down to the eaves of the house. If any one insured were to plant a tree on his property and fail to report the fact to the company within one year, the policy was considered void.

Individually owned fire companies IN these early years, each insurance company maintained its own fire company—not because the city was inadequately prepared in this respect, but because

44

the company wanted to be certain that one company at least would fight the blaze religiously and not be lured into the diversion of a free-for-all before the fire was out. As a consequence, and because of the competitive rivalry between two companies, it was soon apparent that the company which carried the insurance on the burning house was left to fight its flames alone. Had William Penn returned just now, he might certainly have been suspicious of the appropriateness of the name he had chosen for this rapidly growing city, for never was anything more conspicuous by its absence than brotherly love at the time of fire.

WITH the increasing interest in insurance and the many policies in effect, it became rapidly difficult for each company to recognize its own fire. Consequently, the companies adopted what were then known as "house marks," whose use suggests in many ways the merchandising trade-marks of today. And now, when the town bell in Independence Hall would boom an alarm of fire, all of the fire companies would respond, but only the company whose house mark appeared on the house in danger fought the flames. The members of the other companies were the gallery, more inclined to torment the firemen than to assist them.

House marks are adopted

45

The house mark of the Philadelphia Contribution-ship represented two clasped hands, from which the company soon derived the name, carried down even to the present day, of "Hand and Hand." The Mutual Assurance Company adopted as its mark a green tree in full bloom, and thus the name, "Green Tree."

The historical significance of house marks requires more than the meager mention we have thus far made of them, for they were an important, quaint and inter-esting phase of early fire insurance.

What house marks were and how they were put up

KNOWN generally as "house marks," but also known as "fire marks," "badges," "devices," "plaques" and "shields," they originated in Great Brit-ain in 1680, when the "Fire Office" adopted the Phœ-nix, that miraculous bird of immortality, as its design and placed it on all of the buildings which it insured.

In America, the Philadelphia Contributionship was the first company to accept the house mark as the dis-tinguishing sign for the buildings it insured. This com-pany continued the use of its mark until 1870, when the organization of a paid fire department made marks gen-erally useless and quickly obsolete.

The first American house marks were made by John

46

Stow, of Pass & Stow, who recast the Liberty Bell. In their earliest years, the marks were invariably made of lead, with the individual designs of their owners and the number of each policy stamped upon them. Later, copper and iron were used, the latter metal unwisely so because of the ravages of rust and regrettably so because of their disfigurement today.

Usually, the marks were nailed directly on the walls of the insured buildings, although Philadelphia soon asserted her independence again by beginning the practice of first mounting them on wooden plaques or shields about fifteen inches high by eleven inches wide.

Many of the insurance companies which used house marks, finding them expensive to donate to property owners, incorporated in their by-laws some provision to absorb this expense. Thus, from the by-laws of the Philadelphia Insurance Company, whose mark showed a dove, with an olive branch in its beak, perched on an extended hand, we find the following clause: "A badge of moderate cost shall be fixed on every store, warehouse or shop insured, at the expense of the insured, but to be procured and put up by the officer of the company." And in the by-laws of the Fireman's Insurance Company of Baltimore, whose mark represented a circular plate on which was the picture of a hand fire engine and the letters "F. I. Co.," was a clause which read: "The badge shall be charged at $1.25 for its use. No new charge shall be made when insurance is renewed, but if discontinued, badge returns to insuring company."

Clasped hands, Hope, an eagle, a fire plug and other things THE designs adopted for the house marks betrayed, only in rare instances, any sign of originality in their conception. For the most part, they were variations of previously adopted badges, a fact which would lead one to suppose that even in those early years the flattery of imitation possessed more appeal than the hard work of creation. But the marks, imitative or original, had genuine charm and a quaintness that cannot be denied by those who have had the pleasure of examining a collection at close range. Though the motif of two or four clasped hands, which doubtless appealed to those who accepted the definition of Philadelphia literally, seemed to be the most generally used, one does find many other interesting designs:

The Insurance Company of North America, for instance, originally used a six-point navy star, only later to discontinue this in favor of the American Eagle. The

Fire Association of Philadelphia had a mark resembling a fire plug, to which was attached a section of hose and beneath which were the letters "F. A." The Hope Mutual Insurance Company of Philadelphia, which survived no more than six years, adopted a mark depicting the figure of Hope resting on an anchor. The  United Firemen's Insurance Company of Philadelphia used an oval plate on which was shown a steam fire engine and the letters "U. F." This company also had a second mark whose only difference from the first was that the letters "U. F." had been displaced by the words, "United Firemen's Ins. Co." The Lumberman's Insurance Company of Philadelphia, purported to have been  the last company in America to discontinue the use of house marks, had a flat, iron plate on which was an interlaced monogram of "L. I. Co." bordered by four logs of wood.

The designs used by the companies that had been formed in other cities were also interesting and various: The Mutual Assurance Company of New York used what was unquestionably the simplest mark—merely a plain, oval plate containing their firm name and the policy number of the insured. The Baltimore Equitable Society had a square plate with a raised border in which

49

were the conventional two clasped hands. The Pittsburgh Navigation & Fire Insurance Company preferred a heavy, oval plate of iron, with the firm name around the edge and the one word, "Insured," in heavy block letters in the center. The Fireman's Insurance Company of Pittsburgh used a square, iron plate on which was cast a picture of a hand engine. The Penn Fire Insurance Company of Pittsburgh adopted an outline figure of William Penn with the one word, "Insured," in a semi-circle beneath it. The Associated Firemen's Insurance Company of the City of Pittsburgh had a standing figure of a fully dressed fireman in the act of blowing a trumpet held in his right hand, while in his left hand was a wrench for opening fire plugs. All of this arose from an arc of metal inscribed "Fire Company." The Hartford County Mutual Fire Insurance Company used an oval mark of tin on which, in gilt against a black background, was lettered "Mutual Insurance Hartford."

Aside from the reasons we have mentioned for the adoption of house marks, the insurance companies were not long in discovering that they also served an additional purpose that resulted in nothing but general good for the city: They indicated to firebugs, incendiaries,

50

grudge-bearers and revengeful criminals that the owner of the house on which a mark had been placed would not suffer personally by a fire, and that, if caught, their prosecution would be conducted by the insurance company and not by the individual.

There can be no question of doubt that the acts of these parasites diminished noticeably when these facts became generally known.

WITH insurance now an accomplished fact, and with the thoughts of Benjamin Franklin and of other prominent citizens of the day emerging from the chrysalis of theory to the actuality of practice, the year 1752—the year in which the citizens were asked to subscribe to the first Articles of Insurance—gave the history of Philadelphia fire prevention a turn for the better. Fires there still were, of course; but the result of a blaze that mocked all efforts at extinguishment left continually less privation and financial suffering than heretofore—for the assured owner of consumed property could at least watch the last thin thread of smoke with the consoling thought that the insurance company would help him meet the new start that lay before him. *A turn for the better*

THE first fire insurance policy issued in Philadelphia was to John Smith, Treasurer of the Philadelphia Contributionship. The policy covered the Smith dwelling house on the east side of King Street, between Mulberry Street and Sassafras Street—now on Water Street, between Arch Street and Race Street.

Like all other policies then issued, this first policy was protective for seven years only. Under its terms, a certain deposit was required upon issuance of the policy, the deposit being liable to its proportionate share of losses and expenses incurred by the company. Even the interest on the deposit belonged, during the continuance of the policy, to the company; and in the event that the deductions for expenses and losses consumed the full amount of the deposit, a new "contribution" was required to keep the policy in force.

At the expiration of the seven-year term, the assured had the option of withdrawing any balance that Providence or the paucity of fires had left, or of renewing the policy for another similar period under the same conditions.

This seven-year insurance plan, off to a good start at the inception of the country's first fire insurance company on April 13, 1752, remained in effect for fifty-eight years when, in 1810, Perpetual Contracts—and we shall discuss these later—were inaugurated.

WE have seen how quickly the founding of one volunteer fire company led to the founding of others and how quickly the adoption of a house mark by one insurance company led to the adoption of a house mark by another. In the growth of the insurance companies themselves, history again repeats itself and Philadelphia was soon to find itself forging ahead under the inevitable stimulus of competition in the insurance field. *Companies of insurance begin to be founded*

To review the history of these early companies even briefly is to expand the centennial memento of one company into an historical volume of depressing size. Suffice it to record that in December, 1792, the General Assembly of Pennsylvania was petitioned for permission to incorporate the Insurance Company of North America. On April 14, 1794, the incorporation of the company was authorized, and almost immediately thereafter that of the Insurance Company of the State of Pennsylvania. Both of these companies were organized originally to handle marine insurance, but the directors concluded to add the business of fire insurance.

53

THE FRANKLIN FIRE INSURANCE COMPANY, *by a* PERPETUAL CHARTER OBTAINED *from the* LEGISLATURE *in 1829, is* INCORPORATED *and* BEGINS *its* FIRST DAYS *of* BUSINESS.

The Franklin Fire Insurance Company is founded HUMAN nature has forever been famous for its disregard of genius until genius is dead, and many is the man who has not achieved the full glory of his earthly accomplishments until long after death has made him incapable of enjoying that ultimate recognition. It cannot be said that Benjamin Franklin tasted none of the public's acclaim until after his death in 1790. He was famous long before, and his achievements had early brought him the acclaim he well deserved. But it is interesting and significant, in tracing the pattern of fire insurance history through these early Philadelphia years, to find no company being founded as The Franklin Fire Insurance Company until seventy-seven years after the founding of America's first and until thirty-nine years after the death of one of its chief inspirers.

54

The little, old Betsy Ross House, in which the first American flag was made. This was another of the priceless treasures entrusted to the safe-keeping of The Franklin Fire Insurance Company.

RUBICAM'S TAVERN
WAS ONE OF THE
LEADING INNS OF
THE CITY, SITUATED
NEAR INDEPENDENCE
HALL.

55

In 1829, however, due to the untiring efforts of Charles N. Bancker and a quorum of other leading Philadelphia citizens, a perpetual charter was obtained from the Legislature for the incorporation of The Franklin Fire Insurance Company. This was passed by Act of Assembly, approved and signed by Governor J. Andrew Shulze on April 22, 1829. The charter, under state seal, bore the date of May 19, 1829.

A public notice and Rubicam's Tavern

THEN, in the Philadelphia newspapers of the day, public notice was given that the stock-books of the new company would be opened on the morning of May 13, 1829, at the house of Daniel Rubicam, 20 South Sixth Street. No better place could have been chosen, for the house of Daniel Rubicam was likewise known as Rubicam's Tavern, one of the leading inns of the city, situated near Independence Hall in the very heart of the business city. The citizens of Philadelphia, in addition to subscribing to the stock of a company whose founders presaged its success, knew that they might simultaneously subscribe to the excellent ale, wines and liqueurs for which Rubicam was famous. Thus, we find that the entire stock of The Franklin Fire Insurance Company had been fully subscribed the following day.

56

ANOTHER public notice was forthwith inserted in the Philadelphia newspapers, apprising the citizens that the new company had been successfully and fully financed and that, at 10 A. M. on June 8, 1829, there would be held, again at Rubicam's Tavern, the first meeting of the stockholders who would assemble to elect directors.

At this first meeting of the stockholders, Charles Dutilh was selected to act as temporary Secretary and the presidency of the company was offered to Samuel W. Jones who promptly declined to serve because of the pressure of other business which continued to demand his attention. The presidency was then offered to, and accepted by, Richard Willing. Charles N. Bancker was then elected Secretary, and ten stockholders—Richard Willing, James Schott, Samuel W. Jones, Thomas Hart, Henry C. Carey, Thomas I. Wharton, Tobias Wagner, Charles Roberts, Levi Ellmaker and William Chaloner—were elected to serve as directors of the new company.

DURING the company's first business year, two presidents served and two men refused the position—for in October, 1829, Richard Willing declined a re-election. The office was offered to William C. Chaloner who also declined and Clement C. Biddle was named the new president, serving from December, 1829, to October, 1834. Charles N. Bancker, however, who had been so instrumental in obtaining the perpetual charter from the State Legislature, stuck to his post as secretary from that first stockholders' meeting in 1829 to February, 1837, when he was elected president of the company at the resignation of Henry C. Carey. The presidents of the company from 1829 to 1929 are shown in chronological sequence on a separate page in this book.

The so obvious difficulties of filling the presidential chair during the formative years of the company might easily be attributed to the fact that no salary of any kind was paid to the officers, their sole remuneration being in the quantity of food and ale that could be consumed at the regular meetings held in Rubicam's Tavern. A far more likely reason, however, was undoubtedly the fact that each man to whom the position was offered was quite naturally a leading citizen already following some other business pursuit that required his full attention—for it must be remembered that the executives of early Philadelphia days were not in the position of enjoying the same conservation of time that typewriters, adding machines, dictaphones, telephones and automobiles bring to the executives of today.

D ESPITE those early tribulations, however, The *The first ad-* Franklin Fire Insurance Company progressed *vertisement* rapidly, tempering its growth with the conservative policies of an even then conservative community. And as evidence of its business acumen, we find the company advertising for the first time, less than three months after its inception, in no less a medium than *The Saturday Evening Post*. This first advertisement appeared in the issue of August 8, 1829, and read as follows:

INDEMNITY AGAINST LOSS BY
FIRE.
The Franklin Fire Insurance Company of Philadelphia,
Capital $400,000, all paid in.
CHARTER PERPETUAL.

C ONTINUE to make Infurance permanent and limited, on every defcription, of Property, in TOWN AND COUNTRY, on the ufual favorable terms.

Office, No. 163½ Cheftnut street, near Fifth st.
C. N. BANCKER, Pref't.

DIRECTORS.

Charles N. Bancker,	Samuel Grant,
James Schott,	Jacob R. Smith,
Thomas Hart,	George W. Richards,
Thomas I. Wharton,	Mordecai D. Lewis,
Tobias Wagner,	Adolphe E. Borie.

C. G. BANCKER, Sec'y.

THE address is significant, for 163½ Chestnut Street was the property of Stephen Girard, whose philanthropic service to the State is well known in his founding of Girard College; and in the first minutes of the company we find an entry saying that "the Committee on a suitable location reported they had rented of Stephen Girard, Esq., his house No. 163½ Chestnut Street at Twelve hundred dollars for a half year, the rent to commence on the first of July." On June 25, 1829, the company moved into these first offices, but in October, 1844, due to the demands of an increasing business, 163 Chestnut Street, an adjoining property, was also rented. Under the new numbering ordered by the City Councils, these buildings soon became 435 and 437 Chestnut Street; and by 1870, through the increasing value of real estate, the rental had advanced from $2,400 a year to $6,000. On May 1, 1873, the directors purchased the property at 421 Walnut Street which now houses the company.

*Perpetual
Contracts*

ORIGINALLY, and because it was the accepted form of fire insurance of the day, The Franklin Fire Insurance Company had intended to confine its writings to the Perpetual Contracts that, in 1810, had displaced the earlier "seven-year" policies.

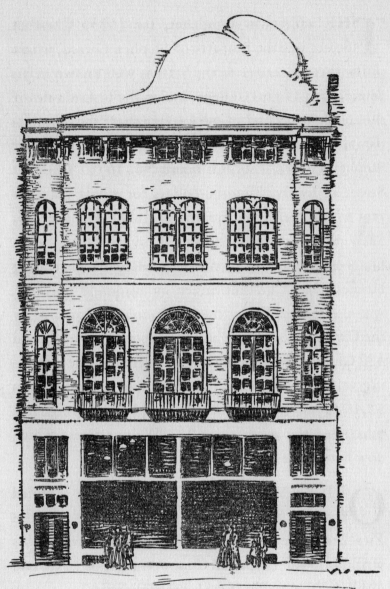

"421 WALNUT STREET"

Perpetual Contracts, as their name so aptly defines, mean simply that the duration of the policy is without limit except by cancellation. These contracts required the deposit of a certain percentage of the face value of the policy, the deposit paying for the policy once and for all and the interest accruing on the deposits proving sufficient to provide for the losses sustained.

A condition of the first "Perpetuals" ALL Perpetual Contracts issued by The Franklin Fire Insurance Company prior to January 1, 1848, were noncancellable as far as the company was concerned, although the deposit could be demanded by the assured if the building was sold. One peculiar condition of the first policies of this sort issued was a provision stating that the contract neither took effect nor was binding if the insured dwelling "was now or hereafter insured in any other office, unless same was allowed by the company and specified on the back of the policy."

The Perpetual Contract remained in force during the time when the insured building was vested in the original owner or in any of his heirs, without assignment of interest from the original owner. In the settlement of a claim under a Perpetual Contract or in can-

Built in 1760 by Chief Justice Benjamin Chew, the old Chew mansion is still in the possession of the family—and still protected by "The Franklin."

celling any such policy, it is frequently necessary, therefore, to have brought to the company by the attorney representing the assured, all papers—in some cases for three or four estates, including copies of the will—so that the assured can properly substantiate his claim for settlement or cancellation.

On the other hand, if a building insured under a Perpetual Contract is sold and the assured does not return his contract within sixty days from the date of the title transfer, the contract becomes automatically void and the deposit, in accordance with the conditions of the policy, is considered "sunk for the benefit of the company," a phraseology still being used even in the new Pennsylvania standard form of Perpetual Contract.

THE early Perpetual Contracts covered any occupancy except certain excluded classes such as apothecary, Queen's ware, flax and hemp, liquors, ship chandler, oils and paints, Windsor chair makers, brewers and malters, soap and tallow chandlers, coach and carriage builders and dealers in varnish. Also a very important warranty to the companies, contained in those early day Perpetual Contracts, was that damage to wall paper would not be covered at a rate in excess of fifty

Certain excluded classes and a warranty

63

cents per piece of paper, and did not in any case include border paper.

Many times in the history of The Franklin Fire Insurance Company losses have been paid under Perpetual Contracts where the rate charged was less than the prevailing annual estimate. Recently, for instance, a total loss was paid under a Perpetual Policy issued on the non-cancellable series, the building at the time of the fire being occupied by a paste company, manufacturing bill-poster sign paste. The term policies paid 60 per cent of the amount of insurance carried by them, due to co-insurance requirements, and The Franklin policy made up the difference.

The origin of the Perpetual Contract IT is not surprising, in view of those earlier "seven-year" policies, that Perpetual Contracts should have originated in Philadelphia with the Philadelphia Contributionship and the Mutual Assurance Company. Their creation was quite natural and obvious, for it was a logical process to agree with the assured to retain his "seven-year deposit" indefinitely, thus extending the term of insurance and making it perpetual.

Both of the original Philadelphia fire insurance companies, and all of the stock companies in Pennsylvania

64

having perpetual charters, have willingly continued the issuance of Perpetual Contracts to the present day, making Philadelphia probably the only city in the country where such policies are still available. New Perpetual Contracts, however, are accepted only on brick or stone dwellings within a radius of ten miles from the corporate limits of the city.

BUT The Franklin Fire Insurance Company, despite its original intention to confine its business to the *A change of intention* writing of Perpetual Contracts, soon found competition and the ever-changing panorama of insurance growth compelling it to issue temporary policies. Perpetual insurance was actively solicited, however, until a great many years later when brokers and agents, under the stimulus of increased compensation, endeavored to sell only term policies, where the commission would be made periodically and not by the small amount of 10 per cent made once in the lifetime of the policy. The income to the company carrying perpetual liability for loss payments is the interest gained from the custody of the money.

Thus, Perpetual Contracts provided the largest percentage of its income to The Franklin Fire Insurance Company for a great many years.

Losses reported under the thousands of old Perpetual Policies still in force in The Franklin Fire Insurance Company are paid today in accordance with the survey which is on file for every early contract, for it is only in recent years that "forms" appear on any of the policies. So many of these records are on hand that a separate basement vault is required for the storage of surveys exclusively.

"The Franklin," indeed, paid its share of the losses suffered in the great conflagrations that have just been recorded; and the amount of these losses has been tabulated, for ready reference, on a separate page.

Applications seriously considered DURING the first year or two of business operation, so many applications for insurance were made to the company that meetings of the directors were held almost daily at 5 P. M. at Rubicam's Tavern. Each application was discussed thoroughly and investigated from all sides and from top to bottom; and many were the applications in those early days that were refused "after due consideration."

"Franklin" issues Perpetual Policy No. 1 THE first applications for insurance were placed before the directors' meeting of July 17, 1829, and the first insurance policy, a Perpetual Contract,

66

The First Continental Congress met in Carpenters' Hall, now a patriotic shrine and one of the notable buildings once protected by a "Franklin" policy.

issued by The Franklin Fire Insurance Company bore the date of July 20, 1829, and had as the assured, one Alexander Henry. This policy covered, in the amount of $2,000 at the rate of 3 per cent, the three-story brick building at 65 North Second Street, "occupied as a picture-frame manufactory." This policy was transferred in December, 1845, to Susan M. Jackson and again, in October, 1856, to Oliver Evans.

As evidence of the necessary conservatism that the company was forced to adopt, and the careful investigation that each application was accorded, the survey for this particular risk, Policy No. 1, filled two sheets of foolscap, starting with the memorandum that the building was 16 feet front by 28 feet, 6 inches deep; that it was three stories high; that the back building was 11 feet, 4 inches deep; that the front door was of double wood with sash bulk jam and held a circular window of 24 lights—and thus, throughout the entire premises, stating the precise thickness and measurement of every single piece of exposed wood.

The cost of this particular survey, in addition to the amount of deposit, was $3.00; and the policy remained in force for sixty years, or until 1889, when the assured received the entire sixty dollars which constituted the original deposit. As no brokerage was known in those days, all contracts were submitted direct to the office of the company.

Perpetual Policy No. 1, however, was not long to remain the company's sole evidence of business income, for very soon thereafter we find The Franklin Fire Insurance Company "writing" many buildings whose historical significance was far more than local. Many of these early policies remained in force for sixty years for the account of the Mayor, Aldermen and citizens of Philadelphia.

Independence Hall IT is interesting to record that one of the earliest "Franklin" policies covered Independence Hall, known to every schoolboy as "the Cradle of American Liberty." It was here, of course, where the Declaration of Independence was drawn up and signed on July 4, 1776; where the Constitution was written and adopted on September 17, 1787; where the Colonial Assembly convened from 1736 to 1775; where the second Continental Congress met; and where George Washington accepted the post of Commander-in-Chief of the American Army on June 16, 1775. The survey which covered this policy records that it also covered the

68

It is entirely fitting and proper that Christ Church, in which Ben Franklin worshipped, should be under the watchful care of The Franklin Fire Insurance Company.

steeple and the clock within it—and it was in this same steeple that the Liberty Bell hung when, to the frenzied joy of all Americans, its deep notes sang the birth of American Independence in 1776.

The Independence Hall policy remained in force for more than sixty years, finally being cancelled when the Council of Philadelphia decided to create an insurance fund for the protection of the historic buildings which faced what became known as "State-House Row." But this early policy, and others of equal historic fascination, remain to this day in the possession of The Franklin Fire Insurance Company.

CONGRESS HALL, which adjoins Independence *Congress* Hall, and which will be remembered as the meet- *Hall* ing place of the first Senate and of the first House of Representatives, as well as the place where, on March 4, 1793, George Washington was inaugurated the first President of the United States and where later he delivered his farewell address, was also covered for many years by a Perpetual Contract issued by this company.

BUT these were not the only risks along "State- *Carpenters'* House Row" that The Franklin Fire Insurance *Hall* Company covered. Carpenters' Hall was soon to be

69

added to the growing list of "Franklin" assureds. This was the building where, as an inscription on the wall so proudly testifies, "Henry, Hancock, and Adams inspired the Delegates of the Colonies with Nerve and Sinew for the Toils of War." Carpenters' Hall will also be remembered as the building in which Parson Duché, on the morning after the news of the bombardment of Boston had presaged the inevitability of war, delivered the famous "first prayer in Congress" to the first Continental Congress. History records that "the old man's prayer brought tears to the eyes of even the grave and passionless Quakers who were present, and the voices which had opposed the proposition to open the sessions of Congress with prayer were never raised for that purpose again."

If the executives of The Franklin Fire Insurance Company expanded with pride when risks of such historical significance appeared on the company's books, the records do not betray it. But human nature being then so slightly different from today, one can readily picture the flowing ale at Rubicam's, in honor of these business coups. "State-House Row," however, as pleasant as the policies that covered it must have been, could have brought no more business satisfaction than other

Erected in 1700, Old Swedes' Church was looked upon in its day as a master-piece of the mason's art. It still stands today, protected by "The Franklin."

policies to follow—and from the standpoint of insuring a building of true antiquity, we point to Old Swedes' Church.

Old Swedes' Church is one of the oldest relics of *Old Swedes' Church* Philadelphia that stands today. It was built in 1700 to take the place of a log structure which had been built in 1677 and which, at that time, served equally well as a place of worship or a place of battle, depending on the rather uncertain humor of prowling Indians.

Christ Church is another famous building appearing on "The Franklin" books. This stands on Second *Christ Church and bells* Street, north of Market Street, on the site of the first church erected by the followers of William Penn. Begun in 1727 and completed by the raising of a steeple in 1753, Christ Church is one of the most impressive monuments to those pre-revolutionary days. George Washington worshipped here, and many were the glorious occasions when the great patriot drew up before its doors in his "gorgeous chariot drawn by four elegant long-tailed bays" and stepped inside through a waiting crowd of his admiring countrymen.

The bells in the Christ Church tower are the oldest chimes on this side of the Atlantic Ocean. They were cast in London in 1754 by Thomas Lester and Thomas

Peck, and were brought to this country, free of charge, by Captain Budden in his ship "Myrtilla."

Ever after, when the captain's ship was spotted coming up the river, the Christ Church bells would chime a joyous welcome.

A tablet in the ringers' room relates that "On Sunday, June 9, 1850, was rung in this Steeple Mr. Holt's celebrated ten-part peal of Grandsire triples, consisting of 5040 changes, in 3 hours and 15 minutes, by (eight performers) being the first peal of change-ringing ever performed in the United States."

To record the interesting buildings insured by The Franklin Fire Insurance Company during the now one hundred years of the company's existence would be a history in itself. One feels, however, in examining the list, that virtually every building of any historic or business significance has, behind the ever-present possibility of its catching fire, a "Franklin" policy to repair the loss.

A meeting of the Board on September 2, 1829　ONE hundred years have now passed since that first meeting of "Franklin" stockholders at Rubicam's Tavern. Each year has been important in the growth of the company; each year has added to its predecessors the increase in business that has rewarded the company with its present strength and size—but, following the fascinating pattern of history back through the years, one realizes that the first—and not the first hundred—year was the hardest. At the meeting of the board on September 2, 1829, four months after the company had been in business, we find in the minutes the following entry: "The Secretary reported that since the opening of the office for business, there had been received $383 on eleven Policies of Perpetual Insurance, $583.23 on 48 policies of Temporary Insurance and that loans on mortgage had been made to the extent of $11,750 at the rate of 6 per cent." This was a good showing for four months of business. Like other insurance companies of the day, however, "The Franklin" was to taste its share of losses.

PHILADELPHIA fires during the Nineteenth Century were—perhaps fortunately so for the insurance companies that were growing gradually during these years—not so devastating as certain of those in other cities. But the insurance companies had by this time written risks in other cities and thus could not look for losses only in their own.

A few Philadelphia fires in the Nineteenth Century

On August 4, 1869, William Patterson's Bonded

Warehouse, at Front and Pine Streets, was burned with a loss estimated at $2,000,000 and with a fatality list of five. . . . On June 5, 1871, in the planing mill of Stanley & Weber, Marshall Street below Girard Avenue, fire consumed literally everything in the block and damaged all the facing residences. . . . On November 6, 1871, the phosphate works of Watson & Clarke, on the banks of the Schuylkill River, near the Gas Works, were burned to the ground. . . . On March 4, 1872, the Jayne Building burned at a loss of $1,500,000. All the fire precautions, such as a system for flooding the floors, and a water pressure machine and hose in the basement, were forgotten. . . . On April 6, 1879, a bad fire occurred in the center of the city. The burned district covered three acres and extended for 300 yards on the north and south sides of Race Street from Crown to Fourth, Thirty properties were destroyed, the fire raged for two days, one man was killed and the loss was $693,500. . . . In 1886 the Egyptian Museum was burned. All the figures were destroyed except a group representing the Crucifixion. As though this were by act of God, the group was photographed after the fire and copies of the picture were sold in large quantities throughout the United States!

THUS reads, on and on, the history of Philadelphia *The paid fire* fires in the years following the incorporation of *department* The Franklin Fire Insurance Company. That these fires were not more disastrous than they proved to be, can, with the exception of William Patterson's Bonded Warehouse conflagration, be attributed in no small measure to the fact that, in 1870, Philadelphia inaugurated the paid fire department that brought to the fighting of fires some semblance of system, efficiency and good deportment. During the paid fire department's first year of service, it is interesting to record that there were 523 fires, a decrease from the previous "volunteer" year of 79 fires and a decrease of $807,-134 in property loss.

Let us also record that the first alarm of fire after the paid department was installed was received at 1.42 A. M. on March 15, 1871, from Box 216. With a mighty cheer from the force and intense excitement among the populace, the city roused itself and rushed pell mell to—a false alarm!

BUT, while Philadelphia was experiencing fires of *Bigger fires* a comparatively minor nature, the country was *in other* soon to gasp in dismay at the tragic conflagrations oc- *cities* curring in other cities, some of which rocked insurance

75

companies to the bedrock of their foundations and threw many into liquidation. And the news from these other cities, worthy of much larger expansion than space will permit our giving it, can be condensed like this:

New York— December 16, 1835 On December 16, 1835, with the thermometer at seventeen degrees below zero, fire broke out in the downtown business section of New York. Many alarms were sounded and finally it was necessary to call upon firemen from Baltimore and Philadelphia to assist. The water, released under tremendous pressure, froze as fast as it left the nozzles of the hose lines. Thirteen acres were burned and ten thousand people were thrown out of employment.... On October 7, 1871, after fourteen rainless weeks, fire broke out in a poor section of Chicago and raged for two days and two nights. The known dead were two hundred. One thousand persons were reported missing. The fire covered an area three miles long by one and one-half miles wide, destroyed 20,500 houses, made 110,000 people homeless and resulted in an estimated loss of $200,000,000! ... On November 9, 1872, Boston was the scene of a great fire which burned for eighteen hours. Sixty-five acres were humbled to ruins, 776 buildings—most of them office buildings—were destroyed, and the property damage was estimated at $85,000,000. A remarkable fact about this fire was that only one life was lost. . . . Both in May and June of 1851, San Francisco suffered two serious fires. One destroyed 2,500 buildings at a total loss of $3,500,000; the other destroyed 500 buildings at a total loss of $3,000,000.

Insurance companies the country over will remember most of those fires. Those which do not remember them were probably liquidated on their account. The Franklin Fire Insurance Company was playing its part in settling losses during these fiery years; but it was also playing its part in obtaining new business and covering the risks that proved more financially effective. But if these fires caused the companies to tremble, the dawn of the Twentieth Century was to bring them two fires for serious meditation.

THE first of these "modern" fires occurred on February 7, 1904, in the city of Baltimore. It began in the basement of the Hurst Building, a wholesale dry goods house with a large supply of celluloid novelties in stock, on the southeast corner of Liberty and German Streets. Within forty-eight seconds after the

Baltimore— February 7, 1904

77

alarm, an engine company and a hook and ladder company were on hand, under the direction of the District Chief. But the blaze seemed of no consequence when the companies reached it, and they used for its extinguishment only a single line of chemical hose. Within a few moments, however, as though the chemicals had fed the fire, the flames leaped through the basement and soon had the entire building ablaze. The result was a two-day conflagration which burned an area covering 140 acres in the business section. Twenty-seven great buildings of fire-resistive construction were gutted and, in some cases, collapsed. The loss was millions, staggering the insurance companies of two continents and sending many of them into bankruptcy.

San Francisco —April 18, 1906 THE second of these "modern" fires caused a loss to insurance companies alone of $300,000,000, when 100,000 policies in 200 companies were filed for claim; and so great was the conflagration that 250 adjusters took five months to complete their work of adjustment! This was the Great San Francisco fire following the earthquakes in the early morning of April 18, 1906. The fires that followed, starting in the business district, raged in an Inferno of more than Dantean

78

fury for three full days and two nights. When the dawn of the fourth day burst with ironical beauty on the smouldering remains of a great city, four square miles of property—the equivalent of 515 city blocks—had been destroyed with a loss so staggering as to be virtually incomputable. Only here and there, like giants in a crowd of Lilliputians, remained any of the familiar architectural landmarks that had made the city's sky-line: 25,000 buildings and their contents had been completely destroyed. And it is interesting to record, because of the evidence of the risks taken by insurance companies of those years, that only 3,000 of these buildings were of brick and steel. The remainder, 22,-000, were of frame construction—open invitations to the ravages of fire.

IN 1831, two years after its inception, the first "Franklin" agency was inaugurated and the company thus became a pioneer in a system of insurance "distribution" that has since grown to tremendous proportions and has networked the entire country. This first agency was planted in Lexington, Kentucky, and John Tilford, a merchant of the town, was formally appointed its first master. *The first Franklin agency leads quickly to others*

The Kentucky agency soon disclosed to "The Franklin" executives that the idea of representation beyond the limited boundaries of their own city was a business producer of no small importance. Thus, we are not surprised to find the prophetic and progressive president, Charles N. Bancker, Esq., perfecting immediate plans for an expansion of the idea, with the result that only a short time had passed before The Franklin Fire Insurance Company enjoyed agency representation in Trenton, N. J.; York, Pa.; Newark, N. J.; Richmond, Va.; Nashville, Tenn.; Baltimore, Md.; Pittsburgh, Pa., and in an ever-expanding number of other municipal-centers.

Nor was the optimism, felt after the success of the senior agency in Kentucky, ill founded, for each agency seemed almost immediately to prove itself a profitable venture. This is a monument both to the integrity of the men selected to head the various Franklin agencies and also to the sagacity of the Franklin executives in their selection.

Charles J. Martin, Esq. THIS brief history would be incomplete without some mention of Charles J. Martin, Esq., the first "Franklin" agent in New York City, who resigned from this company in 1853 to accept a position with The Home Insurance Company of that city. Later, Mr.

Martin became president of the "Home" and, in 1879, was one of the speakers at the banquet given to commemorate the Fiftieth Anniversary of The Franklin Fire Insurance Company.

As an agent for "The Franklin," however, we need record only the statement of affairs of his brief period with this company to record, as well, his exceptional underwriting ability. Mr. Martin's premiums (1849-1850) were $49,782.61. His losses and expenditures were $24,596.63. In other words, Mr. Martin enjoyed a net trade profit of 50 50/100 per cent!

And thus the brief history, during those early years, of a company which now stands high among all the fire insurance companies in the world; whose business extends into every corner of the country, "through Middlesex, village and farm"; which has thousands of agents and agencies throughout the world; whose assets are today more than twelve millions, and which has now, certainly in a pictorial and typographical sense and, we hope, verbally, remembered that the first great chapter of its One Hundred Years of uninterrupted progress has been concluded!

FINIS

Then and Now

Officers and Directors

1829

RICHARD WILLING, *President*
CHARLES N. BANCKER, *Secretary*

Directors

RICHARD WILLING	THOMAS I. WHARTON
JAMES SCHOTT	TOBIAS WAGNER
SAMUEL W. JONES	CHARLES ROBERTS
THOMAS HART	LEVI ELLMAKER
HENRY C. CAREY	WILLIAM CHALONER

1929

CHARLES L. TYNER, *President*

CLARENCE A. LUDLUM, *Vice Pres.*	WILFRED KURTH, *Vice Pres. & Treas.*
HAROLD V. SMITH, *Vice Pres. & Secty.*	FRANK E. BURKE, *Vice Pres. & Secty.*
VINCENT P. WYATT, *Secretary*	HARRY H. SCHULTE, *Asst. Treas.*
FERD. ERMISCH, *Asst. Secretary*	JOHN GLENDENING, *Asst. Secty.*

Directors

FRANK E. PARKHURST	JOSEPH M. STEELE
JOSEPH A. STEEL	THOMAS WRIGGINS
CHARLES K. YUNGMAN	J. WILLISON SMITH
CLARENCE A. LUDLUM	OWEN J. ROBERTS
CHARLES L. TYNER	WILFRED KURTH
WILLIAM IVES WASHBURN	HAROLD V. SMITH

82

PRINTED IN U. S. A. BY
FRANKLIN PRINTING COMPANY
PHILADELPHIA